What Ca... with the Elephant House?

Miriam Gaynor and Aleshia Goodwin
photographs by Adrian Heke

Contents

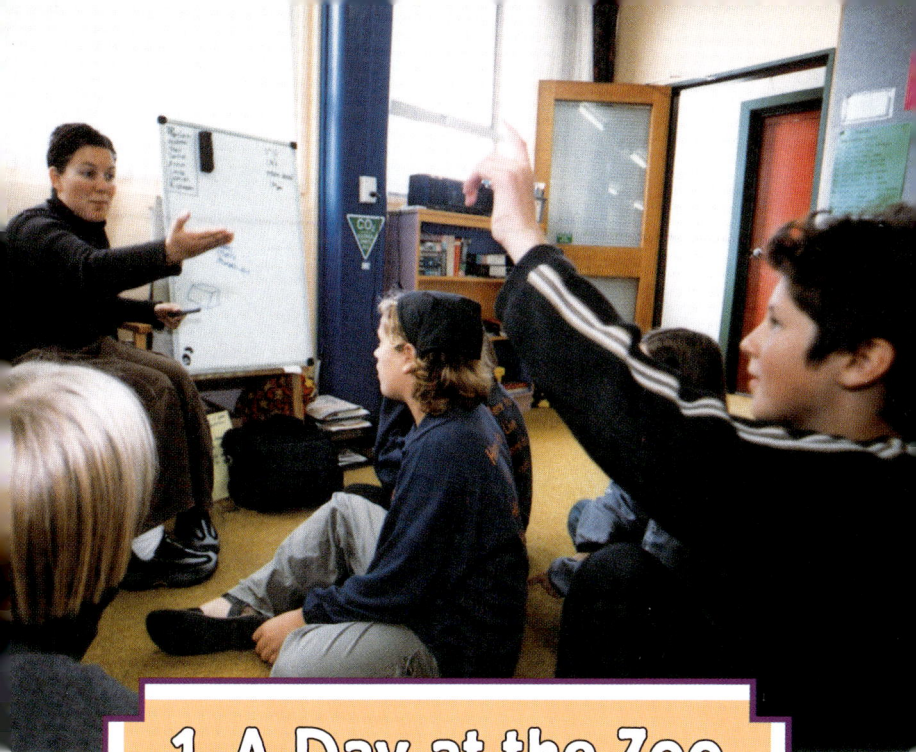

1. A Day at the Zoo

It all started with a school visit to the zoo. The summer holidays were coming up, but our teacher, Miss Baker, thought that we still had time for one more class project. We'd been studying how to plan a project and present a "proposal".

Setting Out a Proposal

A proposal is a very clear way of writing down your ideas for a project so that someone else can easily understand what you are suggesting and decide if they think that it's a good idea. There are five questions you can ask that will make sure that you have thought of everything.

What?

Write a clear description of your project and the expected results.

Why?

Describe your reasons for doing the project.

Who?

List the people who will need to be involved and in what ways.

How?

Describe the practical steps required to carry out the project.

Work out how much money will be needed and where it will come from.

When?

Prepare a timeline for the project, matched to the steps.

Different groups were going to different places round the city to look for project ideas. Miss Baker suggested that some of us go to the City Zoo. Maybe we could choose an animal and think of some way to improve its environment. Or maybe we'd think of some other project. Then, back at school, we'd write up our idea as a proposal.

It was fun visiting the zoo. But thinking of ways to improve things for the animals wasn't easy — the zoo takes good care of its residents. We did come up with a few ideas, though. One was to put more trees and plants in some of the enclosures. Another idea was to set up an obstacle course for the hamsters so that they would have a more interesting way to get their daily exercise.

When all the groups got back together at school, we had a great time talking through our ideas with Miss Baker and then making posters of our proposals.

2. Real Projects

The really interesting part came a few weeks later. The zoo educator called our school and asked if we'd like to do some *real* projects for the zoo — not just presenting proposals but carrying them out as well!

So we were off to the zoo again. The idea of doing a project in the community was exciting — and a bit scary too. People would get to see what we'd done! We talked about the things that we'd need to keep in mind — our "project boundaries":

"It mustn't cost too much."

"We have to be able to do most of the work ourselves."

"We don't have a lot of time before the holidays, so it can't take too long."

"We have to be able to finish what we start."

Another group came up with the idea of building a bird house and feeder to hang in a tree. It would give birds a place to rest and maybe to nest. Good idea!

We couldn't think of any way to improve things for the animals, so we decided to think about people instead. We tried to think of something that might make a visit to the zoo more fun or help people to see something that they might miss. We came up with three "possibles".

Follow Me to the Bison

Some of the animals were quite a long way from the entrance, and not many people were visiting them. We could paint footprints on the paths leading to their enclosures. That may make people want to walk that little bit further and see the bison for the first time.

Picture Signs

Some of the signs at the zoo are in words. Adding a picture of the animal to the sign might make it easier for younger children and people who don't speak English to find their way about.

LEOPARDS >

Elephant House Café

We noticed an unusual building right in the middle of the zoo that nobody seemed to be using. The sign said "Elephant House", but we couldn't see an elephant. Come to think of it, we couldn't remember having *ever* seen an elephant at this zoo. Why not? (Don't all zoos have elephants?)

The building was old and a little run-down, but it had a kind of magical feel about it. Right away, we decided that our project would be to find a use for it. It would make a cool café!

3. Where Have All the Elephants Gone?

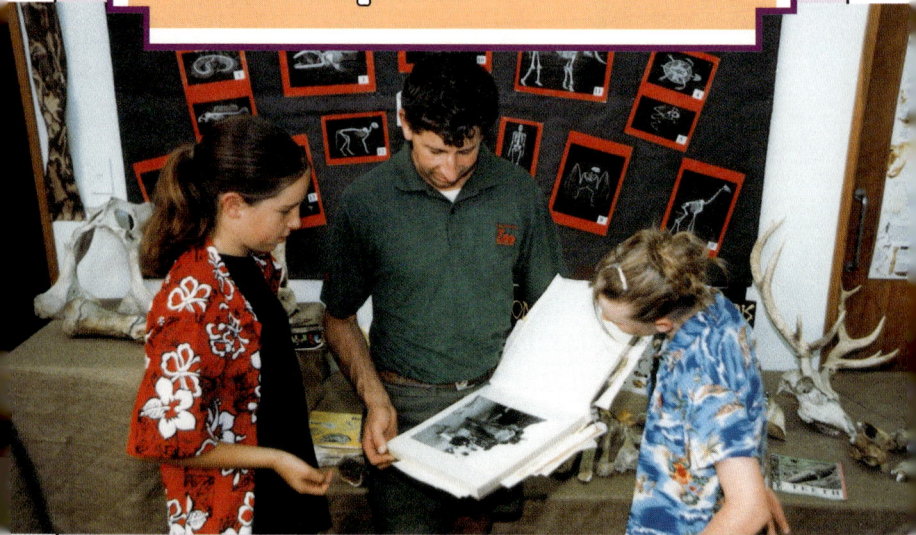

First, we wanted to find out more about the elephant situation. We learnt that one of the zookeepers, Ron Goudswaard, had lots of books with all kinds of clippings, photos, and information about the history of the zoo and its animals. We arranged to visit him.

THE ZOO

This is Nellikutha, the City Zoo's first elephant, with her keeper. The Elephant House was built for her in 1927. It really was her "house" – she had her showers, ate her meals, and slept there. During the day, she was taken outside to walk about, and sometimes she gave people rides round the zoo. She died in 1945.

We asked Ron why there's no elephant at the zoo now. He told us that when the last elephant, Kamala, died in 1983, the City Zoo decided that they couldn't just replace her with another single elephant.

Modern zoos try to give their animals a more natural environment to live in than the animals have had in the past. And since wild elephants live in herds, not on their own, it's best to have a group of at least two or three living at a zoo.

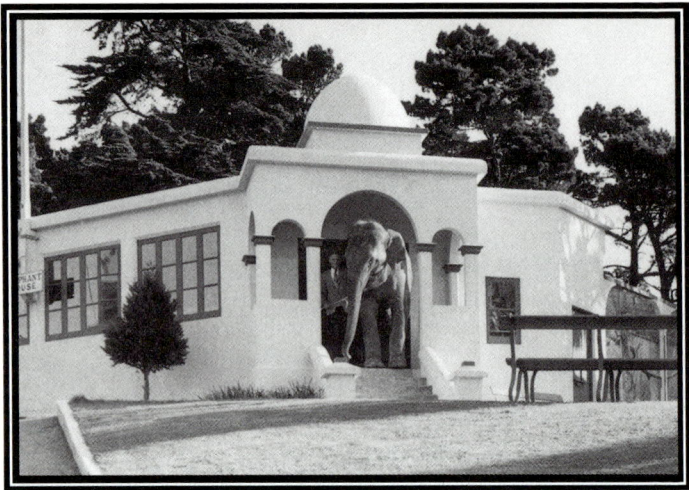

The Elephant House in 1952, with Maharanee in the doorway.

Getting and keeping that many elephants would cost lots of money and take up lots of space. The zoo decided that it would be better to use their resources to make things better for all the other animals already living at the zoo. So that's why we'd never seen an elephant and why the Elephant House was now just a storeroom. We thought that using it as a café would be a much better idea!

Nellikutha giving an elephant ride. Today, many zoos believe that it's not appropriate to use animals in this way.

4. Brainstorm

We needed to talk our Elephant House idea over with someone from the zoo, so we went to see Jean Pugh, the zoo educator. She teaches at the Zoo School, where kids come to learn more about the animals and how they are cared for.

After talking about our plan for the Elephant House with Jean, it became clear that setting up a café would be too difficult. We'd need licences, equipment, furniture, and staff. We knew that the zoo couldn't give us that sort of money, and we couldn't see how we could raise it ourselves. We remembered our project boundaries: is it low-cost, can we do the work ourselves, can we finish it before the holidays? The café idea didn't fit with any of them.

We felt sad about giving up on the Elephant House because we thought it was a cool building with an unusual history. Then Jean said, "If you really want to find a use for the Elephant House, why don't you brainstorm all the possibilities?" So we did! Then we discussed each idea with Jean and added comments to our notes.

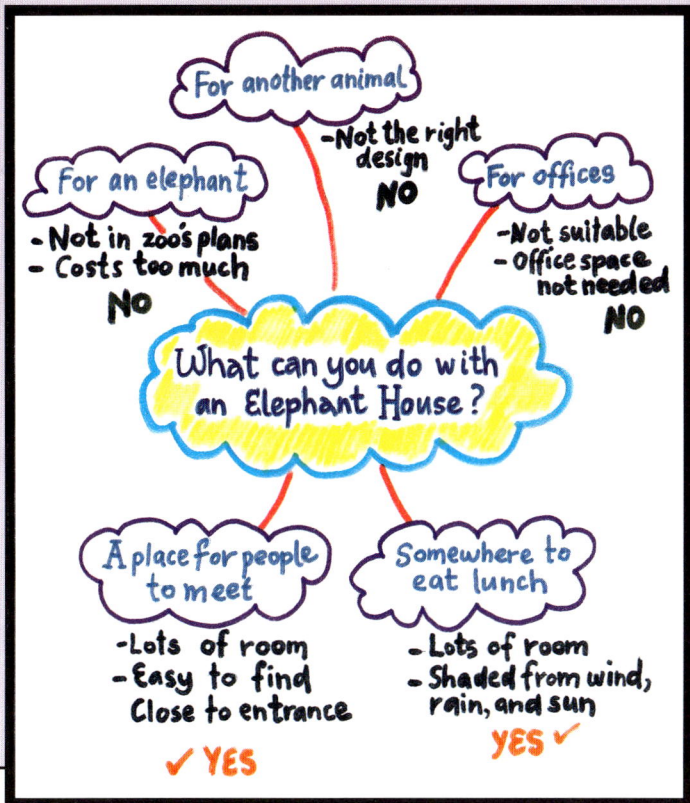

For another animal
-Not the right design
NO

For an elephant
- Not in zoo's plans
- Costs too much
NO

For offices
- Not suitable
- Office space not needed
NO

What can you do with an Elephant House?

A place for people to meet
- Lots of room
- Easy to find
Close to entrance
✓ YES

Somewhere to eat lunch
- Lots of room
- Shaded from wind, rain, and sun
YES ✓

Our brainstorm helped us to see that even if we couldn't set up a café in the Elephant House, the building could still be useful. It would make a great place for school groups and other people to get together before they set off round the zoo or to sit and eat their lunch out of the wind or sun.

This seemed like a project that we could start and finish!

Back at school, we made a detailed plan of our project, using our teacher's five questions:

1. What? (Expected results)

We would like to make part of the old Elephant House at the zoo into a pleasant space where people could meet and sit and eat their lunch.

2. Why? (Reasons)

• The Elephant House is an interesting building, and it's easy to get to. It's a waste to use it as a storeroom.

• People could use the new space to sit and talk, to rest, or to eat their lunch on hot, windy, or wet days.

• It would help us to learn more about carrying out a community project, and we would learn a lot of skills along the way.

3. Who? (People involved)

• Ask the zoo's management about using equipment to do the job and money needed to complete the job.

• Talk to zoo staff about the history of the Elephant House.

• Call paint shops to get the best deals on paint.

• Organise free time with Miss Baker to make wall hangings and do painting at the zoo.

• Miriam and Aleshia: We'll do most of the work.

4. How? (Action)

- Remove the things that are stored in the Elephant House at the moment.
- Find money for paint and materials.
- Clean and paint the main room.
- Put in tables and chairs.
- Add colourful wall hangings and displays.

5. When? (Time frame)

We only have a few hours each week for the project. It has to be finished before the summer holidays.

First week – measure the room, price the materials, find the best deals.

Second week – empty the room and clean it, start making hangings and displays.

Third week – paint the walls, complete the hangings and displays.

Finally, we wrote a letter to the zoo manager about our idea, faxed it off to the zoo, and crossed our fingers.

5. Getting the Green Light

A couple of days later, the zoo manager, Alison Lash, sent us a return fax saying that she liked our idea. She suggested that we come and take a closer look at the building before we presented our proposal. Great!

We began to realise what a challenge we'd taken on.

There were some display cases along one wall, but they were mostly empty. We thought that it would be good to have some fish or frogs or insects in the empty ones.

The first thing we had to do was to draw a detailed floor plan and measure the walls in the main room. This would help us work out how much paint we'd need.

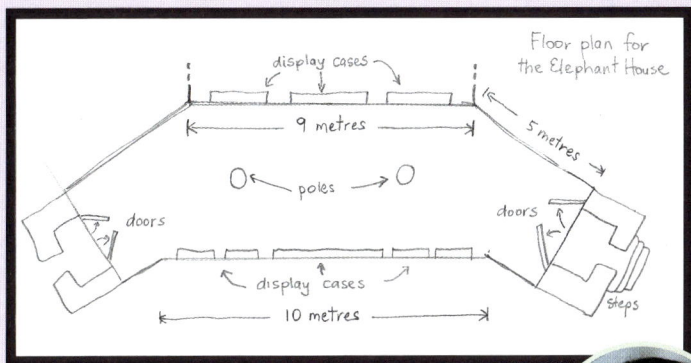

Floor plan for the Elephant House

display cases

9 metres

5 metres

O ← poles → O

doors

doors

display cases

10 metres

steps

We went away and did a lot of telephoning and calculating, working out the costs for all of our ideas. The main cost would be paint, so we called a lot of paint shops and found the cheapest deal. Finally, we wrote out our proposal and sent it off to the zoo. The next day, they faxed it back with their feedback.

Proposal 1

We would like to make part of the old Elephant House into a pleasant space for people to meet and sit and eat their lunch.

We propose to:

- clean and paint the inside of one of the rooms yellow and red to match the zoo colours, with some green too

  There isn't much money for this project. Maybe you could use cheaper paint or fewer colours? Our painter may be able to help. The zoo will paint the outside of the building.

- brighten the place up (put in more windows?)

  Adding windows: It will be too costly.

- have displays of fish, frogs, and insects in the tanks along one wall

  Frog or insect displays: There is no budget to look after them. A cold-water fish display could be possible.

- have a display of elephant and historical photos

  Elephant display: Sorry — we don't want people to think that there's a chance of getting elephants back at the zoo.

- put in some tables and chairs

  Tables and chairs: Yes — we have some that you can use.

- have some background music.

  Music: It will be too difficult to wire up the room.

We will do the work ourselves and finish it before the summer holidays.

We had to rethink our plans. We sent in our revised proposal.

Proposal 2

We would like to make part of the old Elephant House into a pleasant space for people to meet and sit and eat their lunch.

We propose to:

- clean and paint one of the rooms; work to be done by us with help from the zoo painter

- have a tank of fish and some non-living displays in the other empty display cases

- put in some tables and chairs

- brighten up the room with painted wall hangings made by us.

We will finish the work before the summer holidays begin.

The zoo liked our second proposal. We had the green light!

6. Messy Work

Deciding what we actually could do had taken a lot of time. Miss Baker told us that this stage of a project usually does. There are always more things to find out and discuss than you expect, and then there are all the changes to make to your plans. But now we had to get on with the work in a hurry. The holidays were getting close! We made a list of our tasks:

Things to do and things we need

* Clean walls and doors – bucket, cloth, and detergent
* Sweep and clean floor – brushes, bucket, mop
* Paint walls – rollers, brushes, paint, ladder
* Design and paint wall hangings (at school) – paint, paper
* Clean out display cases – brush, cleaning stuff
* Put up wall hangings
* Have zoo put in tables and chairs

The list didn't look very long, but everything seemed to take more time than we expected. By the time we'd washed and dusted and swept, we didn't have a lot of time left for painting.

We got lucky with the paint, though. When we told the paint shop about our project, they gave us some free!

We decided that we wanted a bright colour for the walls because there wasn't much light coming into the room. We had a lot of white paint and a tin of bright yellow. We mixed them together and ended up with a nice, warm yellow colour. Just right.

Then came the really hard part – the painting. The zoo painter wasn't available to help us after all, but the zoo let us use some of their painting equipment. It took us five hours to paint all the walls. Some of them were made of concrete, and it took two or three coats to cover the rough patches. The brushes and rollers flicked paint everywhere. We must have looked like we'd just had a very messy paint fight!

Whenever we had free time back in class, we worked on our wall hangings.

Miriam did a frilled lizard with the sun rising, and Aleshia decided on a leopard asleep in a tree.

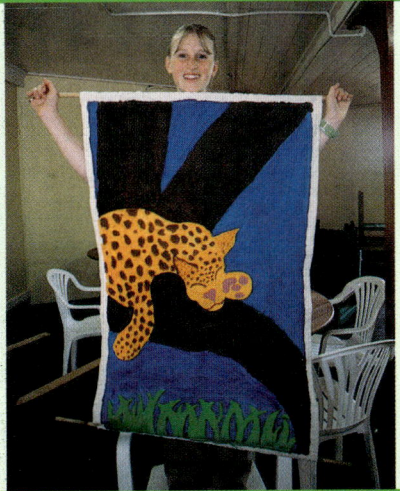

We put up the wall hangings, and they looked perfect against the yellow walls. Jean also gave us some posters and students' work from the Zoo School to display.

7. The Doors Are Open

At last our new-look Elephant House was ready. What a great feeling! We felt as if all our hard work had paid off.

When we looked back at our proposal, we saw that we'd done nearly everything we had started out to do. And we sure learnt a lot about planning and working on a real project in the community. It was time well spent.

Now the doors to the Elephant House are open. The zoo has painted the outside of the building and trimmed the bushes. It looks great.

Inside, visitors to the zoo can sit down at the tables to rest and talk or to eat their lunch. The zoo gardener has set up some displays in the cases along one wall — old gardening tools, postcards that show what the zoo and its animals used to look like many years ago, and all sorts of interesting things that have been dug up or found at the zoo.

And there's a TV monitor that lets you see right inside the tiger enclosure. You can watch a tiger and her three new cubs.

We thought of Nellikutha and wondered what she'd have thought about people sitting down and eating sandwiches in *her* house. We decided that she'd think it was a great idea too.